STUDY-AID SERIES

Notes on T. S. Eliot's

MURDER IN THE CATHEDRAL

Methuen Educational Ltd

LONDON · TORONTO · SYDNEY · WELLINGTON

First published in 1965 by
Methuen & Co. Ltd
Reprinted 1969, 1971 and 1975
by Methuen Educational Ltd
11 New Fetter Lane, London EC4P 4EE
© 1964 College of Careers (Pty) Ltd
Printed in Great Britain by
Fletcher & Son Ltd, Norwich

ISBN 0 416 48790 4

All rights reserved.
No part of this publication may be reproduced, stored in a retrieval system, or transmitted, in any form or by any means, electronic, mechanical, photocopying, recording or otherwise, without the prior permission of the publisher.

NOTE: These Notes are published for use as an aid to the study of English Literature for examination purposes. It is important to remember that the Notes serve only as an aid to the study of the book and do not in any way relieve the student of the necessity of reading the original text.

CONTENTS

THE AUTHOR AND HIS WORK

BIOGRAPHY

THOMAS STEARNS ELIOT was born in 1888 in the large industrial and commercial city of the United States, St. Louis, where his father held a major position in the local business world; on both sides of his family, the author of *Murder in the Cathedral* is descended from seventeenth century New England settlers. And it was this family tradition which sent him to Harvard University in Massachusetts, where he spent four years (1906-10) studying philosophy and literature.

Thereafter, he studied further in Germany, in Paris, and at Oxford. Finding himself in England during the First World War, he became a schoolmaster, married in 1915, and soon afterwards joined the staff of Lloyd's Bank in London. It was during this period that his poetic work began to appear in various magazines, some of which he edited himself (*The Egoist*, 1917-18; *The Criterion*, 1923-39). In 1925 Eliot became a director of the firm of Faber & Gwyer, now Faber & Faber, who have since published all his literary output.

With the publication of *The Waste Land* in 1922, Eliot established his reputation as a poet, and for the next ten years his influence in the world of letters was at its height. In 1927 he became a British subject and announced in the preface to a book of essays his conversion to Anglo-Catholicism.

In the late 'thirties he entered upon a more mature and mellow phase, began to be widely acclaimed by the more traditional and conservative literary circles, and formal recognition of his stature as a writer came in 1948 with the award of the coveted honour, the Nobel Prize for Literature.

From this point onwards T. S. Eliot was a world figure in literature. He published comparatively little but lectured widely in Europe and America. His fame—which he regarded with wry amusement—was based, often for the wrong reasons, mainly on *The Waste Land* and *The Cocktail Party* but his best work was done in criticism. It is said that the fees he received for his lectures, especially in the United States, were higher than any lecturer had ever before been paid.

In 1957 he married for the second time, his first wife having died in 1947, and his last years were the happiest of his life. He died in January 1965.

Eliot's literary work falls into three principal categories: (i) poetry; (ii) critical essays; (iii) verse-drama.

His first major poetic work, as already stated, was *The Waste Land* (1922), a satirical attack on the lack of firm foundations in modern civilization, a work which was hailed as a most convincing presentation of social aimlessness – after forty years, however, the piece has lost a good deal of its impact. After turning to Anglo-Catholicism, he struck a note of quieter religious acceptance in *Ash-Wednesday* (1930), though the sense of annihilation recurs and the imagery remains far from simple. In his two other major poetic works, *The Rock* (1934) and *Four Quartets* (1944), he made use of mystical writers, like St. John of the Cross, to present a mood of restrained penitential hope and faith.

Eliot's critical essays appeared in *The Sacred Wood* (1920), *The Use of Poetry and the Use of Criticism* (1933), *Essays Ancient and Modern* (1936), *What is a Classic?* (1945), and *Notes toward the Definition of Culture* (1949). This body of critical prose is an indispensable introduction to his poetry – especially because, compared with his verse, his prose is lucidity itself. Nonetheless, in these essays he writes as if he is breaking new ground for the first time, explaining what nobody has previously thought of; in reality, most of the views he expresses were commonplace in the nineteenth century; many of them are to be found in the essays of Matthew Arnold!

However, his critical writings were widely read and greatly admired among scholars, especially at the universities, because, whether "new" or not, they made people *think*. At a time when literary criticism was otherwise undistinguished – in England, at least – Eliot offered a solid body of clear and erudite work, and at least in one field, the study of Dante, his criticism was original and enlightening.

Murder in the Cathedral (1935) was the first of a series of highly successful verse-dramas, to be followed by *Family Reunion* (1939), a study in the psychology of guilt, *The Cocktail Party* (1949), an exploration of social trivialities, *The Confidential Clerk* (1954), which was first produced at the Edinburgh Festival, and, most recently, *The Elder Statesman* (1959), which also had its first public performance at the Edinburgh Festival before going to London.

LITERARY AND IDEOLOGICAL BACKGROUND

Eliot's intellect was developed before the First World War at universities with strong traditions. He was also much influenced by the prophetic books of the Bible and the esoteric teachings of Zoroaster and Buddha. By training and temperament, therefore, he was something of a mystic.

At the same time he had a practical man's aptitudes and experience in business, and was fully alive to the contrast between nineteenth century culture and twentieth century material civilization with its mechanization and extreme forms of division of labour – and especially the human types these seemed to produce. Moreover, while in London and Paris, he had had the opportunity of first-hand contacts with symbolist poets like Amy Lowell and Ezra Pound, whose approach favoured an attitude of detachment and impersonality.

With this background, Eliot set himself the task of evolving a new literary technique which was also to owe a great deal to the developments then taking place in the field of psychology. Recognizing that the human brain works by the association of words or ideas, one current flowing into another, the subconscious blending or conflicting with the conscious, with reason trying to hold the balance and fix the attention, Eliot developed the technical device of the Internal Monologue. This is virtually a one-party dialogue between two halves of the same person, each at variance with the other, in which the reader enjoys the luxury of observing the workings and conflicts in the character's mind.

Eliot also felt keenly that modern verse was suffering from a lack of standards. It was bound to benefit from the studied felicities of Elizabethan drama with its emotional intensity and vivid phraseology. He had learnt a great deal, too, from studying Dante, a writer whose graphic and unconventional approach keeps alive the attention of readers or audience.

Viewed in retrospect, T. S. Eliot is essentially a philosopher whose thoughts have been expressed in poetry and verse-drama.

Section II

HENRY II AND THOMAS BECKET

MURDER IN THE CATHEDRAL deals with the assassination of Thomas Becket, Archbishop of Canterbury, at the instigation of King Henry II in December 1170. Accordingly, it is necessary to have some background knowledge of the historical circumstances in which the play is set.

CHARACTER AND TEMPERAMENT OF THE KING

Henry II of England, born in A.D. 1133, ruled from A.D. 1154 to his death in A.D. 1189.

We know a great deal about him because he lived in an age when it was fashionable to comment on the activities of kings; and Henry impressed his contemporaries so strongly that they could not refrain from saying what they thought of him. Those close to him feared his occasional outbursts of wild anger and were exasperated by his unpredictable activity. Peter of Blois, one of Henry's courtiers, has left a vivid account of the constant uncertainty experienced by the king's followers — "and if the king promises to spend the day anywhere, especially if a herald has published the royal will, you may be sure that the king will leave the place bright and early, and upset everyone's calculations in his haste. You may see men rushing madly about, urging on the pack-horses, fitting the teams to their wagons; everyone in utter confusion — a perfect portrait of hell."

But the king's perversity and sudden changes of plan were not the only qualities which had impressed Peter of Blois. Elsewhere he fills out the picture. The physical description is famous: the hair once reddish, now turning to grey, of middle height, round-headed, his eyes brilliant as lightning when roused, his deep chest, strong arms and bow legs. The courtier then goes on to give an account of Henry's remarkable qualities as a leader and ruler, and of his special interests. "He is an ardent lover of the woods: when he is not at war, he amuses himself with hawks and hounds . . . As often as he has free time he occupies himself in private reading or expounds some knotty problem to his clerks."

In fact, Henry II was the first English king after the Norman Conquest to be fully literate. He had been well tutored as a young man; he liked

4

to have learned men about him; he was curious about history and literature; many treatises were dedicated to him – a sign that his patronage was generously given.

Much of his reign was spent in France, where the Plantagenets held vast dominions; when he was not warring and organizing his possessions on the Continent, his main object at home was that of all the Norman kings – to build up the royal power at the expense of the barons and of the Church. On the whole, Henry – for the period – was an able and enlightened sovereign, a clear-headed but unprincipled politician, and an efficient general; during his reign he introduced several great legal reforms.

BECKET'S EARLY CAREER

The most powerful man in England after the king was Theobald, the old Archbishop of Canterbury. Relations between them were outwardly cordial, and Henry rarely refused an urgent request from that ecclesiastical leader. The most striking indication of Theobald's influence was the presence of his favourite clerk and archdeacon, Thomas Becket, in the office of royal chancellor and in the most intimate counsels of the king.

Becket, born in London in A.D. 1118 of Norman parentage, came from a family of wealthy merchants. He was trained in knightly exercises, studied theology in Paris, and worked for a time in a lawyer's office. About A.D. 1142 he had entered the household of Theobald, who heaped honours on him (including the archdeaconry of Canterbury, A.D. 1154) and sent him on several important Continental missions. At the papal court Becket had supported Henry's claim to the succession to the throne, and, in return, a year after Henry's coronation, he was rewarded with the office of Chancellor (A.D. 1155), thereby becoming the first Englishman born since the Conquest to fill any high office of state.

Henry himself, it is clear, felt that the Church had acquired the habit of acting more independently than was fitting; and he was anxious, once Theobald died, to replace him with a man who would be less independent, a useful adviser, and a welcome ornament of the court. Such a right-hand man seemed to be available in the person of Becket. As Chancellor, Becket had revealed a mixture of efficiency and glamour; here was someone who could maintain the pageantry and organize the details of the court, and yet be wholly subservient and congenial to the king.

In A.D. 1162 Theobald died, Becket became the new Archbishop of Canterbury, and there was little to suggest that the cordial relationship between Henry and Thomas would alter.

In actual fact, from that date, Becket tried to establish an entirely new relationship with the king. The worldly Chancellor became an aescetic monk and prophetic spiritual leader. The more Becket acted out of character (as Henry understood his character), the more irritated the king became. A series of minor disputes swiftly developed into a major quarrel. At last, in A.D. 1164, Henry determined to break the new Archbishop.

In January of that year, at Clarendon, he tried to secure Becket's consent to a catalogue of essential customs governing the relationship between Church and State. The Constitutions of Clarendon were a solemn affirmation of ancient practice (rather than new laws) and Henry browbeat Thomas and his colleagues into assenting to them.

Becket soon repented of his submission at Clarendon and put himself at the mercy of the Pope. In October the Archbishop went to Northampton, where he had been summoned to face trial before the king on several of the points of issue between them; but whatever the nominal grounds for the trial, the real question was whether the Constitutions were binding and whether Becket himself was to continue in office. At Northampton Becket refused to submit to trial, claiming total exemption from the jurisdiction of the royal court, and fled the country. Behind this breach lay a whole world of ideas and assumptions in which the lay and clerical views diverged. And beyond this lay the tragedy of an intimate friendship translated into a bitter quarrel. Henry's view of the matter was comparatively straightforward: he had trusted Becket implicitly, and Becket had let him down; the Archbishop had sworn allegiance to the king, broken his oath, and was thus a traitor.

Why had Becket behaved in this manner? Thomas was only too well aware that, at the time when the king had forced the monks of Canterbury to elect him archbishop, he was widely regarded as a time-serving royal minister, who would continue his old way of life even as Archbishop of Canterbury. Above all, he knew that the older bishops regarded him as a caricature of an archbishop – as a royal plaything. So circumstances induced Thomas to make some effort to convince the world that he was going to try to be a real archbishop, not too unworthy a successor of his old master, Theobald; above all, he needed to dispel the illusions of the king. Perhaps he also felt the need to convince not only king, bishops and old associates, but also himself, for Becket was a complex personality whose character remains something of an enigma.

At the end of A.D. 1164 the exiled archbishop laid his case before the Pope, Alexander III, who was a distinguished canon lawyer and a wily diplomat. Becket was something of an embarrassment to him, since he already had a war with the Holy Roman Emperor on his hands. Until A.D. 1170 he managed to restrain the archbishop's occasional outbursts of violence; then, with a much more favourable international situation, the Pope took sterner action.

Behind the scenes the old clerical rivalry between York and Canterbury played a significant part. By custom, the Archbishop of Canterbury alone had the power to anoint and crown a new English king, and this custom was supported by a papal mandate to protect Canterbury's rights while Thomas was in exile. But Henry was impatient to have his eldest surviving son (another Henry) crowned as successor in his own lifetime, and ordered the Archbishop of York and his colleagues to crown the young prince. In June, A.D. 1170, this ceremony was duly performed at York, and Archbishop Thomas, with the Pope's support, immediately threatened an interdict (i.e., an order closing all the churches in the kingdom). The grave consequences of such an action on a mediaeval state made this threat too strong even for Henry II, who immediately patched up a reconciliation.

Shortly afterwards Becket received papal authority to excommunicate the bishops who had assisted in the coronation. After a spell of indecision, Thomas published this order and the next day (December 1st), returned to England. On Christmas Day, from his pulpit at Canterbury, taking for his text "peace on earth to men of goodwill", Becket cursed those who had pillaged his estates during his six-year exile – "may their memory be blotted out from the company of the saints". (Eliot omits this altogether from his version of the sermon.)

Meanwhile, at his Christmas court near Bayeaux, Henry, who had been informed of the excommunication bill, became violently angry, and the king's furious question – why no one would rid him of this low-born priest – was answered. On the 29th December four knights, who had just crossed from Normandy, threatened the Archbishop in his palace and on his defiance followed him, with cries of "king's men", into the cathedral, and there, at vespers, after an effort to drag him from the church, killed him with their swords before a crowd of witnesses.

CONSEQUENCES OF BECKET'S DEATH

Few events in mediaeval history shocked the conscience of Europe so profoundly or so immediately. Becket's death was followed by whispers that miracles could be performed at his tomb; these reports became so insistent and widespread that the Pope was moved to canonize the murdered archbishop.

After this, even Becket's arch-enemy had to submit. As an act of penance, in A.D. 1174, King Henry was compelled to walk barefoot through the streets of Canterbury and to submit to a flogging from the monks of Canterbury Cathedral. In due course numerous churches were dedicated to Thomas's name in many remote parts of Britain and Europe.

But the long-term practical effects of the murder in the cathedral were somewhat less dramatic. Although the Constitutions of Clarendon were abrogated, most of their clauses remained quietly in effect and on all crucial issues between State and Church fresh compromises were found. Yet, for a time, appeals to the Pope became more frequent in England than anywhere else, so that the ultimate victor was neither the Crown nor Canterbury but Rome.

As for Henry himself, he never again exercised that compelling force at home or on the Continent which had previously made all his antagonists assume opposition to be futile. Having been publicly humiliated, he had lost some of his personal magic in an age which still was both romantic and highly superstitious.

INTRODUCTION TO THE PLAY

STAGE HISTORY

M URDER IN THE CATHEDRAL, a poetic drama in two acts, had its opening performance in June, 1935, in the Chapter House of Canterbury Cathedral, only a few yards from the site of the spot where Archbishop Thomas Becket was murdered in A.D. 1170. The part of the martyred Thomas was played by the actor Robert Speaight, and the production was in the hands of E. Martin Browne.

Eliot himself told a friend (William Turner Levy):

> I cannot conceive of the play being done on a conventional stage. It is not, after all, a commercial venture. I wrote it to be performed in Canterbury Cathedral as a religious celebration, and so I would always prefer that it be performed in a consecrated setting. I do not know why anyone would want to see it as entertainment.

But in this he was strangely and utterly mistaken. When the play was transferred to the public theatres of London and New York it immediately proved its stage-worthiness. In London it ran for more than a year at the Mercury Theatre and since these first productions it has continued to be performed and to exercise a widespread influence.

The first reaction of the drama critics was to hail *Murder in the Cathedral* as "a work better fitted than any other twentieth century composition to mark the foundation of a modern poetic theatre" (Allardyce Nicoll) and as a reanimation of a dramatic form "which in England has been dead or dormant for nearly three hundred years" (*The Spectator*).

VERSE-FORM

In actual fact, Eliot was not anxious to copy the poetic conventions found in the plays of Shakespeare and perceived that (to quote the author himself) — "a form which has been perfected by one age cannot be copied exactly by writers of another age. It belongs to its own period. If we wrote in the dramatic form and in the versification of Shakespeare we should only succeed in making rather poor imitations of Shakespeare: we

9

should not be contributing anything to the life of our own time . . ."
("The Need for Poetic Drama", *The Listener,* 25th November, 1936.)

Accordingly, Eliot's poetic form in this play, though usually iambic (as in Shakespeare), avoids blank-verse, and secures variation by making frequent use of effective triple measures and internal rhymes, with the punctuation at natural breathing pauses to make delivery easier. (See also Section VII.)

OUTLINE OF THE ACTION

In Part I, news comes to the people of Canterbury that the exiled Archbishop has patched up a reconciliation with the king and is returning home. When the Archbishop arrives, however, he is confronted by Four Tempters who remind him of his former deeds and temporal powers and suggest various means by which he can obtain power and glory.

In an Interlude Becket preaches a Christmas sermon in which he reminds his congregants of the paradox of Christmas, and he has clearly chosen to leave himself in the hands of God, to face martyrdom.

In Part II, on the fourth day after Christmas, the people of Canterbury have forebodings of doom; four knights accuse Becket of ingratitude to the king and later burst into the cathedral, slaying the Archbishop on the chancel steps. The murderers then step out of character and present their side of the story to the audience. The cathedral priests, however, are aware that God has now given "another saint to Canterbury".

FILM VERSION

In 1951 Eliot made considerable additions and alterations to the text for the production of a film by George Hoellering; for this screen version the author also selected the cast, the background music, and approved the costumes and sets. The film kept to the original outline of the action until after the murder of Becket; then, to preserve continuity, the crowd is shown storming the cathedral and the knights have to act quickly and decisively to save their skins instead of addressing the audience at leisure (as on the stage).

The film version had its world première at the Venice Festival, where it received the prizes for the Best Film in Costume and the Best Art Direction; however, when subsequently released for general circuit, it attracted relatively small audiences and was not a box-office success.

MODEL ANSWERS TO QUESTIONS ON

MURDER IN THE CATHEDRAL

Question 1: Recount the happenings in the Archbishop's Hall on December 2nd, 1170, from the time the Chorus is attracted to the cathedral precincts until the women are rebuked by the Second Priest.

Model Answer to Question 1:

In the Archbishop's Hall, adjoining Canterbury Cathedral, a *Chorus* of poor local women has gathered, drawn by some irresistible power to witness some act the nature of which remains as yet unknown to them.

The Chorus laments the passing of the seasons from bountiful autumn to death-like winter with its hardships, and has premonitions both of imminent treachery and of martyrdom. The women reflect that it is now seven years since the Archbishop fled from Canterbury; he had always been kind to the common people, but they fear that things will not go well with them should he return; though they have been oppressed by both the king and the barons during his exile, for the most part they have been left to their own devices and they are anxious to remain undisturbed. Nonetheless, only God controls future events – and these they must await as passive witnesses.

Three Priests attached to the cathedral then enter the scene and speak of the ceaseless intrigues and meetings abroad between the Pope, Archbishop Becket, and "the stubborn king" (Henry II), commenting on the duplicity of secular rulers whose prime motivation is "greed and lust" for power.

Their conversation is interrupted by the arrival of a *Messenger* with the news that the Archbishop has returned to England and is approaching the outskirts of Canterbury; they are to prepare to meet him. He adds that Thomas has been received with frenzied enthusiasm by the people en route. But to the priests' anxious questionings about Becket's relations with the king, the messenger replies that the two proud men have not had a genuine reconciliation – some sort of truce has been patched up between them and it is his opinion that this will not last.

The First Priest recalls how Becket, as Chancellor, though flattered by the king and fawned on by courtiers, had always been too proud to stoop

11

to their level; impartial, generous, and personally virtuous, Thomas recognized only God as his superior. Had the king been a weaker character, or, alternatively, had he been great enough to overlook his former Chancellor's pride, their bitter quarrel would never have arisen.

The Second Priest is pleased that the Archbishop has returned. He will be able to give them firm guidance, to dispel their doubts, and to withstand the encroachments on the powers of the Church by the landowners and barons. He urges his companions to meet Becket with thanksgiving. The Third Priest comments that during the Archbishop's exile the wheel of fortune has stood still and no progress has been made either in the direction of good or evil; he is glad that this static position has now ended and that the situation is to be resolved one way or the other.

But the Chorus of Women is certain of impending doom. The applause greeting the Archbishop's return preludes his death and a time of trouble for everyone. They do not wish to be drawn into the feud between Church and State and to be trampled underfoot in the process. They hope that Thomas will see reason before it is too late and return to France before any damage is done.

The Second Priest rebukes the women for their foolish, immodest babbling, and urges them to forget their craven fears and join in "a hearty welcome to our good Archbishop".

Question 2: What occurs from the time of Becket's arrival in Canterbury until he realizes what his future course of action is to be? (Pay particular attention to his encounters with the Tempters.)

Model Answer to Question 2:

Thomas Becket, Archbishop of Canterbury, enters Canterbury and meets the priests and the assembled women. He has overheard the women's words of fear and declares that there is much wisdom in what they have said; but God regulates our actions and we must submit to His will; the Archbishop implies that his return to Canterbury has not been a matter of personal choice and that they must all await its outcome with fortitude.

The Second Priest apologizes for their meagre welcome, but the Archbishop's seven years of exile has been a period of emptiness for them all and they have had plenty of opportunity to prepare their hearts for this great day. He promises to install fires in Thomas's rooms, since, accustomed now to a better climate abroad, the Archbishop is sure to feel the chill of the English December.

Although grateful for their kind attention, Becket expects to have little rest or leisure in Canterbury. The rebellious bishops, who have supported the king against him, have tried to intercept letters from the Pope (suspending them for participating in the coronation of Henry's son); during the whole of his return trip he has been surrounded by spies; and on landing at Sandwich he would have been molested by his waiting enemies had they not been warned by the Dean of Salisbury that action against the head of the church is treason. Nonetheless, they will continue to hover like hungry hawks, waiting an opportune moment to attack.

The *First Tempter* enters, reminding the Archbishop of the old carnal pleasures he had once enjoyed as "gay Tom Becket of London". Now that the king and he have reconciled their difference, Becket should be prepared to allow both clergy and laity to relax "in mirth and sportfulness". Thomas says only a fool believes that he can put back the clock. The Tempter thereupon reminds Becket that in former times he was less hard on sinners and infers that now he should be prepared to "leave well alone". As the First Tempter cheerfully takes his departure, Thomas reflects that "leave well alone" is a delusion which diverts the mind and prevents one from devoting all one's attention to the problems of the present.

The *Second Tempter* comes to tempt Thomas with secular power: he points out that when Becket was made archbishop he should have retained his post of Chancellor, in order to protect the poor, to strengthen the rule of law, and to prevent abuses of power – doing God's work in a practical way – even though it would also have meant submission to the whims of the king. The Tempter urges Thomas to reassume the position of Chancellor; Henry spends much of his time waging war on the Continent and would be glad of a firm deputy ruling for him at home. Thomas's answer is that, with the support of the Pope, he (as Archbishop) possesses the keys of heaven and hell; as the country's supreme spiritual power, why should he stoop to punier duties? But the Tempter, denouncing the Archbishop's pride, reminds Thomas that he is no more than a "self-bound servant of a powerless Pope", a ruler without a realm, trapped in Canterbury like a hunted stag. After the departure of the Second Tempter, Thomas reflects that once he would have been glad to seize the opportunity of promoting the country's welfare through exercising temporal power – but to do so now would mean descent from a loftier spiritual plane.

The *Third Tempter* arrives – a plain-spoken "country-keeping lord who minds his own business". The blunt-speaking member of the baronial class tells Thomas that he has no hope of any genuine reconciliation with King Henry and urges him to throw in his lot with the barons against the Crown; such a coalition would strengthen the hand of the Church, extend the influence of the Pope, and end Henry's tyrannous jurisdiction over the barons. Proudly, Thomas reminds him that, as Chancellor, he (Becket)

13

had ruled the nobles like "an eagle over doves" and he refuses now to betray the king.

Left alone, the Archbishop reflects, however, that he has often thought about joining the barons to depose Henry; yet, though Samson had used his strength to destroy the Philistines as well as himself, Thomas, if he should destroy himself, resolves not to break anyone else in the process.

The Archbishop is now joined by the *Fourth Tempter*, and is taken aback, having expected only three visitors. This Tempter urges Becket to pay no attention to the plans of his previous visitors: it is most unlikely that the king will ever fully trust him again and the barons, seeking only private advantage, will never be united against the king. In any case temporal power is an ephemeral thing which is continually crumbling under the weight of fresh conspiracies and broken pledges. Thomas, however, holds in his hands the reins of everlasting spiritual glory: by seeking the way of martyrdom, the Archbishop can win an enduring crown which future ages cannot tarnish. Then, as a saint in heaven, Becket will be able to look down at his persecutors suffering timeless torment in hell. Thomas recoils from this suggestion, but the Tempter points out that he is simply repeating what the Archbishop himself has often dreamt of and echoes Becket's own thesis that action and suffering are synonymous.

Thereupon the Chorus comments on the oppressive atmosphere and the Four Tempters declare that the life of man is nothing but a series of disappointments: achievements lack substance and existence itself becomes increasingly divorced from reality. Becket, they continue, has deceived himself with the delusion of his own grandeur; a victim of his own great pride, he is obstinately bent on self-destruction and has become not only the enemy of society but the enemy of himself. The Three Priests urge the Archbishop not to fight the irresistible current of adversity but to await a more favourable turn of the tide.

Then, Chorus, Priests, and Tempters, alternately, refer to the impossibility of warding off death by taking advance precautions: "Death has a hundred hands and walks by a thousand ways." The women, directly addressing the Archbishop, recall that they too have known suffering but have learnt to accept affliction when it comes and to hold together as well as they can the pieces left of their broken lives, all the time trusting in God; but now God appears to have forsaken them and the Lords of Hell are bent on destroying both Becket and everyone else.

Thomas now realizes that his future course of action is clear. He reflects how the Fourth Tempter, in urging him to "do the right deed for the wrong reason", had suggested the greatest treason of all. He recalls the course of his own life: how he had once taken a delight in music and philosophy and games of skill and danger; once these youthful energies were expended, he had become ambitious, serving the king as warrior and statesman. He had not wanted to become a servant of God, for the servant of God stands in greater danger of sin than does the layman, and spiritual issues are not easily divorced from political ambitions. Addressing the audience, Becket stresses that the Tempters are now finally defeated and that his course is to submit himself entirely to the will of God and to await with a humble heart whatever decision God may choose to make. There is no escaping from one's sins by consciously seeking the way of martyrdom.

Question 3: Give a brief outline of the main points touched on by the Archbishop in the course of the sermon he delivers on Christmas morning.

Model Answer to Question 3:

On Christmas morning. A.D. 1170, the Archbishop delivers a sermon in Canterbury Cathedral, taking as his text "peace on earth to men of goodwill" (Luke XI: 14).

Becket tells his congregation that his sermon this Christmas morning will be a short one. He wishes them to meditate on the deep mystery of Christmas, since it is a time when both the birth and the death of Christ are celebrated — a time of joy and mourning; this is a strange paradox indeed.

He then goes on to explain the Christian meaning of peace: it does not embrace the popular conception of quiet satisfaction with the material state of things; instead, it implies spiritual peace; Jesus sent forth his disciples to suffer torture, imprisonment, and disappointment, but, at the same time, to experience the inward peace of doing God's will.

The Archbishop continues by pointing out that the day after Christmas is celebrated as St. Stephen's Day, for Stephen was the first Christian martyr. Accordingly, here again is mourning and joy combined: we lament over the death of the blessed Stephen but we rejoice that another soul is numbered among the heavenly saints.

True martyrdom, Becket explains, can never be the result of a man's will to become a saint; a true martyr is one who has surrendered his will, who submits himself entirely to the will of God and does not even covet the glory of becoming a martyr.

In conclusion, Thomas refers to Archbishop Elphege, an eleventh century martyr of Canterbury, and hints that the city may soon have another martyr, himself. He asks them to consider carefully the significance of his words.

15

Question 4: What occurs in the Archbishop's Hall on December 29th until the priests forcibly drag Becket into the cathedral?

Model Answer to Question 4:

The Chorus of Women laments the barrenness and cold of winter and refers to the vague but oppressive atmosphere of death which overhangs everything. The season of peace and goodwill, they continue, has little meaning unless men are prepared to keep the peace of God. They look forward to the bustling activities of the spring season, but they fear that these activities will hide some great wrong committed in the interim.

In turn, the three Priests then enter: the First speaks of St. Stephen, the first martyr, the Second refers to the Feast of St John the Apostle (December 27th), and the Third to Holy Innocents' Day (December 28th); their remarks are interspersed with appropriate Biblical quotations. Then, standing together, with the banners of the saints behind them, they discuss the holiness of the fourth day after Christmas – now already "half gone" – which as yet has no memorable event to celebrate. The Third Priest suggests that December 29th may yet prove a momentous day.

The Priests are joined by *Four Knights* who tell them that they are servants of the king just arrived from France on urgent business with the Archbishop. The First Priest offers them a meal before they see Becket, but the Knights rudely brush aside this hospitality and insist on seeing the Archbishop immediately. An attendant is sent to summon Thomas, who arrives a few moments later.

On seeing the Knights, Thomas, sensing his impending doom, remarks to the Priests that, however certain one is that a particular event will happen, its arrival may still take one by surprise. The Knights insist on speaking to the Archbishop alone, and Becket dismisses the Priests. Then, in chorus, the Knights charge Thomas with treacherous behaviour against the king after accepting honours from Henry. Becket used the powers conferred on him for his own ends and broke his oath of allegiance. Thomas hotly denies these accusations and refers to himself as the king's "most faithful vassal in the land".

When, in mocking tones, the Knights offer to pray for Thomas, he asks them if they have merely come to scold and blaspheme or if their business with him is more specific. In rage, they make as if to attack him, but the Priests and attendants return and quietly interpose themselves.

The Knights then accuse Thomas of stirring up trouble in the king's French dominions and of turning the Pope against Henry. Yet Henry offered clemency, made a truce with the Archbishop, and restored him to all his honours and possessions. But how has Becket repaid this charitable behaviour? By denying the legality of the young prince's coronation and suspending from office those bishops who had crowned the prince. The

16

Knights say they have been sent to summon the Archbishop to the king's presence to answer these charges.

Becket replies that the suspensions were carried out on the orders of the Pope and that he has no intention of again being separated from his congregation by being forced abroad. Angrily, they accuse him of insulting the king and he retorts that they are guilty of defying the judgment of Rome.

The Knights declare that the Archbishop's words confirm his treacherous and treasonable behaviour, and as Becket leaves the hall, they brush aside the Priests and pursue him with their swords drawn.

The Chorus, sensing that the Knights are "death-bringers" and that the murder of Thomas is imminent, recognize that they will be involved in the sin of the murderers. The spirit of evil is abroad and everything has become horrible and unnatural. And, since evil is indivisible, it is shared by all created things. The Chorus calls upon the Archbishop to forgive them.

Thomas returns and comforts them with the assurance that even the evil of their timid inaction will be turned into a good for themselves and all men through the martyrdom which God has ordained. The knowledge of the weakness to which man succumbs springs out of the remorse which accompanies the consequences of such weakness, and this knowledge is the beginning of wisdom and grateful recognition of the love of God.

The Priests urge Thomas not to waste time in talking: the Knights are coming back and will surely kill him; they plead with him to flee to the altar. Thomas, however, refuses to take flight since death will only come to him when God considers him worthy of it. But the Priests insist that he shall not absent himself from the evening service, and when the Archbishop refuses to accompany them, they forcibly drag him off into the cathedral.

Question 5: Carefully recount the circumstances surrounding the murder of Becket.

Model Answer to Question 5:

As the moment of martyrdom approaches, the Chorus has a vision of horror beyond all horrors that life can bring – the ultimate horror of the separation from God at the Day of Judgment, the horror of the Void. There is no escape from God's silent servant, Death, and nothing to divert the soul from the fear of what comes after.

Meanwhile, inside the cathedral, the Priests have barred the doors since the Knights are like ferocious beasts who will show no respect for the sanctity of church property; when Becket says that he will not have a sanctuary turned into a fortress, they reply that, just as one is entitled to protection from wolves, so also should one be able to protect oneself from "beasts with the souls of damned men". Becket, however, will depend on no material aids: the Law of God is above the Law of Man, and victory is to be gained through suffering and not by stratagems or physical resistance. Accordingly, at his insistence, the doors are opened and the Four Knights, now slightly drunk, enter the cathedral.

Using the Biblical phraseology of a Negro spiritual, the Knights call upon Becket, "the meddling priest", to join them, while the Priests urge the Archbishop to seek refuge in the crypt. Not only does Becket hurl defiance at his persecutors by refusing to resign as Archbishop, to absolve the clergymen he has excommunicated, and to renew his obedience to the Crown – he also turns on the First Knight, Reginald FitzUrse, and accuses him of being a traitor to his feudal oath of loyalty to the Archbishop, and to the Church. The Knights advance to the chancel steps and attack Becket; he dies with the name of God and the blessed saints on his lips.

At the moment of the murder, the Chorus declares that the whole world is made foul by the enormity of the sin now being committed. They feel separated at last from the petty safety of everyday existence and recognize that they share the sin of the world which necessitates Thomas's sacrifice. At first the blood of Thomas seems to defile the land, their beasts, and themselves. They see it as symptomatic of their guilt, linking them to the murderers. Yet the women vaguely perceive that Thomas's sacrifice will cleanse the universe.

Question 6: (a) Describe the Knights' arguments in justification of their murderous behaviour. (b) Give a brief resumé of the play's closing action after the departure of the Knights.

Model Answer to Question 6:

(a) The Knights, having completed the murder, advance to the front of the stage and address the audience in the manner of a series of after-dinner speeches. The First Knight admits that their action may appear contrary to the English sense of fair play, but requests a hearing for their side of the case. As chairman, he calls upon the Third Knight, Baron William de Traci, to open their case.

The Third Knight stresses that they themselves do not stand to benefit or profit at all from the murder: in fact, for reasons of state, King Henry will probably disassociate himself from the whole business and they will have to spend the rest of their lives in exile. Nonetheless, though they had the greatest admiration for the Archbishop as a person, it was their duty to put him out of the way.

The chairman then calls upon Hugh de Morville, the Second

18

Knight, who is a specialist in statecraft and constitutional law. He begins his speech by appealing to the audience to view the whole business soberly and level-headedly and not to be taken in "by emotional clap-trap". He recalls how the king had hoped to strengthen the effectiveness of the central government by combining in one man the two posts of Chancellor and Archbishop. But what had happened? Immediately, Becket had resigned his temporal position and had become "more priestly than the priests" – thereby frustrating all efforts to curb the pretensions of the Church. Thus, by the previous speaker – how Becket completely reversed his effective means of parliamentary censure) they have served the interests of all citizens, and if there is any guilt the audience must share it with them.

Richard Brito, the Fourth Knight, re-emphasizes the point made by the previous speaker – how Becket completely reversed his policies after becoming Archbishop, becoming indifferent to the country's welfare and a victim of his own egotistical pride. He had used every means of provocation, determined to seek death by martyrdom by deliberately kindling their righteous anger; in short, the only verdict that can be returned, Brito insists, is that Becket committed suicide while of unsound mind.

With a final injunction to their listeners to disperse quietly and not to provoke any disorder, the Four Knights take their leave.

(b) The play resumes its former course and the First Priest laments Becket's death: they have lost their guide and protector, the Church lies prostrate and vulnerable to attack and the unbelievers will triumph. But the Third Priest declares that the Church itself is triumphant in this adversity and will retain this moral supremacy as long as men are prepared to die for it; as for Becket's murderers, they can travel to the far corners of the earth, seeking escape in material pleasures or in natural adversity, but their guilty consciences will never allow them any real solace.

The Priests draw consolation from the fact that God, through Becket's martyrdom, has given another saint to Canterbury.

As a choir in the distance sings a hymn in Latin, the women gather together and resolve into a significant pattern the recurrent images of their previous chants – the seasons, beasts and birds, the everyday tasks, the blood of redemption; all these things, they declare, fit together in the scheme of God's Providence. By the blood of redemption fertility is restored to the barren land so that the rhythm of the seasons can remain undisturbed, the natural order can be preserved, men can perform their seasonal tasks and give articulate praise not just for themselves, but for the beasts as well, and all creatures are secured in their ordained places, fulfilling their rôle in the eternal design. They acknowledge that Thomas's sacrifice was made on their behalf and that, under the impact of his martyrdom, they have moved from apathy and evasion to a lively faith and humble acceptance.

Striking a final note of joy, the Chorus stresses that nothing in the future can remove the sanctity of the holy spot where Thomas met his death; they thank God for conferring such a blessing on Canterbury and call upon the martyred Becket to pray for them.

TEXTUAL NOTES

NOTES TO PART I

p. 11 **no safety in the cathedral:** the precincts of church property in mediaeval times provided sanctuary for those seeking escape from urban, feudal, or royal prosecution.

presage: an omen, something that foretells a future event.

p. 12 **All Hallows:** the festival of the saints (1st November).

deny his master?: a reference to the denial scene in Jesus' trial. before the Sanhedrin when "the Lord turned and looked on Peter" (Luke, XXII, 53-67).

Seven years: it is now December A.D. 1170; Becket had left England in A.D. 1164.

p. 13 **our Sovereign Lord the Pope:** i.e. the Priests do not recognize Henry II as their overlord and owe their allegiance directly to Rome.

p. 14 **malversation:** appropriating public property for private ends.

circumlocution: the use of unnecessary words.

p. 16 **prognostic:** a sign or omen of some future event.

p. 17 **temporal devolution:** conferred by secular (i.e., non-ecclesiastical) authority.

p. 18 **Until the grinders cease:** one of the metaphorical images from the closing section of the Book of Ecclesiastes, XII, 3-5.

p. 19 **living and partly living:** this recurring phrase and the descriptions in between reflect the tremendous struggle on the part of the mediaeval peasant communities to scrape a subsistence living from the soil with rudimentary tools and unscientific methods of farming, but harried by recurrent crop failures, famine and pestilence.

p. 21 **They speak better than they know . . . :** these words of the Archbishop are to be thrown back at him by the Fourth Tempter later on (cf. p. 40).

p. 22 **prevision:** foresight.

Sandwich: one of the original Cinque ports on the Kentish coast (now silted-up), 11 miles east of Canterbury.

Broc, Warenne: two of King Henry's supporters who had denounced Becket as a traitor; Warenne, in fact, was the King's half-brother.

p. 24 **viols:** mediaeval stringed instruments—larger predecessors of the modern violin.

p. 26 **Clarendon:** a village near Salisbury (Wiltshire), scene of the passing of the Constitutions of Clarendon (A.D. 1164), which had aimed at securing supremacy of state over church.
Northampton: after abrogating the Clarendon Constitutions, Becket had been summoned to this town to stand trial at a royal court.
Montmirail: a town in the Plantagenet province of Maine (north-west France) where Becket had patched up a truce with Henry before returning to England.

p. 29 **churl:** contemptuous term for a serf.

p. 32 **the Angevin:** Henry II; the Angevin dynasty included the Plantagenet kings down to Richard II; the name was derived from Henry's father, Geoffrey, Count of Anjou.

p. 34 **in the tilt-yard:** in the jousting arena; Becket had fought in France and had unhorsed many an opponent.
Samson in Gaza: a reference to the Biblical incident (Judges, XVI, 15-31) when the mighty Hebrew, Samson, was taken prisoner by the Philistines, blinded, and subsequently destroyed their temple (and himself) at Gaza.

p. 38 **the shrine shall be pillaged . . . :** this and subsequent references are to the dissolution of church property by Henry VIII and his successors during the English Reformation.

p. 41 **parturition:** the act of bringing forth, of giving birth.

p. 44 **against Toulouse:** Becket refers to King Henry's campaigns in France (1159-60) in which he himself (then Chancellor) had also participated.

NOTES ON THE INTERLUDE

p. 47 **oblation:** an offering to God.

p. 48 **"Peace I leave with you . . . ":** these words by Christ and those subsequently quoted in this paragraph are taken from John, XIV, 27.

p. 49 **the blessed Stephen:** Stephen's famous speech and the circumstances of his death are recounted in Acts VII.

p. 50 **Elphege:** Archbishop of Canterbury, who died when the Danes sacked Canterbury during one of their frequent raids on Kent in the early 11th century; his martyrdom is traditionally said to have taken place in the year A.D. 1012.

NOTES TO SCENE 1, PART II

p. 54 **Princes moreover did sit . . . :** Psalm CXIX, 23.

p. 55 **Introit:** a psalm sung as the priest approaches the altar.
In the midst of the congregation . . . : a reference to the preaching of St. John; the words which follow are from the First Epistle, I, 1-3.
Out of the mouth of very babes . . . Psalm VIII, 2.
In Rama: Jeremiah, XXXI, 15.

p. 56 **As for the people . . . :** John, X, 11.

p. 59 **The papers in order . . . :** Thomas has been attending to official Church business and has left all his documents in order.
his jack: the King's odd-job man.
Cheapside: in the heart of the City portion of London, between Newgate and Cornhill; it was in this district that Thomas was born in A.D. 1118.

p. 60 **vassal:** subject of a feudal overlord.

p. 63 **anathema:** the formal pronouncement of excommunication.
evince: to show.

p. 64 **absolve:** forgive, pronounce not guilty.
mendicant: beggar belonging to a clerical order.

p. 65 **attainting:** accusing of criminal behaviour.
malfeasance: illegal conduct by a public official.

p. 66 **subtile:** finely-woven, extremely thin.
jerboa: a small mouselike rodent.

p. 67 **ingurgitation:** greedy swallowing.

p. 69 **minster:** church of a monastery; or, important church, cathedral.

p. 70 **vespers:** the evening service.

NOTES TO SCENE 2, PART II

p. 70 **a Dies Irae:** mediaeval Latin hymn ("The Day of Wrath"), but something of an anachronism here as it was composed only in the 13th century to be chanted at burial services.

p. 73 **the lion, the leopard, the wolf:** cf. Jeremiah, V, 6.

p. 74 **Come down Daniel . . . :** a reference to the story of the prophet in the lions' den, Daniel, VI, 12-23.

p. 75 **arrogated:** assumed without legal right.

p. 76 **blessed martyr Denys:** bishop of Paris who died a martyr's death in the year A.D. 280.

p. 80 **the late Queen Matilda:** Henry I's only daughter who married Geoffrey of Anjou in A.D. 1128, by whom she became the mother of Henry II; she died in A.D. 1167.

the unhappy usurper Stephen: nephew of Henry I who usurped the throne after his uncle's death in A.D. 1135 but was forced (A.D. 1153) to acknowledge his own nephew (Henry II) as his successor; he died at Dover in A.D. 1154.

p. 84   the Gates of Hercules: the classical name for the Straits of Gibraltar.

p. 85   Te Deum: a hymn of praise to God, supposed to have been composed by St. Ambrose in the 4th century.

p. 87   coast of Iona: one of the islands of the Inner Hebrides off the west coast of Scotland.

the canal: another anachronism—in mediaeval Europe and Britain artificial waterways were virtually unknown, those built during the Roman era having fallen into decay.

Section VI

"TEST YOURSELF" QUESTIONS

(WITH ANSWERS)

THE following short or one-word-answer questions range over the factual contents of the whole play. The answers should be written down and then checked with the correct list at the end of this section, but no attempt should be made to tackle these questions until the text of the play has been carefully studied.

Award yourself two marks for each perfectly correct answer (being especially careful about the proper spelling of names of characters and places). Over eighty per cent indicates a sound knowledge of the play's contents; sixty per cent to eighty per cent is good, fifty to sixty per cent mediocre to fair, and less than fifty per cent denotes that further intensive revision is essential.

1. On what date does the action of Part I of the play take place?
2. For how many years had Becket been away from Canterbury?
3. According to the opening chorus, when winter comes what will it bring with it?
4. According to the messenger, what sort of truce had been arranged between King and Archbishop?
5. What were Becket's last words to King Henry?
6. What, according to the Second Priest, do the women of the Chorus resemble?
7. What is the first line spoken by Becket in the play?
8. What comfort does the Second Priest promise the Archbishop?
9. Which two bishops supported the rebellious Archbishop of York?
10. At which port had Becket landed from France?
11. Who saved Becket from molestation from his enemies after he arrived in England?
12. What does the First Tempter have to say about friendship?
13. How many years late, according to Thomas, is the First Tempter?
14. Where had Thomas accepted constitutions which had limited the clergy's powers?
15. At which English town had Thomas been summoned for trial by a royal court?
16. Where in France had the Archbishop and the King apparently reached a reconciliation?

25

17. Who asserted that: "Power is present. Holiness hereafter."
18. Who was the Third Tempter?
19. From whom were the Third Tempter and Thomas descended?
20. What name was given to the family to which Henry II belonged?
21. Over whom did Thomas once rule "like an eagle over doves"?
22. Which Biblical figure provides Thomas with an example of "The desperate exercise of failing power"?
23. Who, according to the Fourth Tempter, will Thomas see "far off below . . . where the gulf is fixed"?
24. What "has a hundred hands and walks by a thousand ways"?
25. What, according to Thomas, "is the greatest treason"?
26. Where in France had Thomas once fought on Henry's side?
27. From which of the New Testament gospels does Becket take the text of his sermon?
28. Who was the first Christian martyr?
29. To which martyr of Canterbury does Becket refer in the course of his sermon?
30. Which bird, according to the Chorus, "rehearses the hollow note of death"?
31. Before whom is the banner of St. John the Apostle carried?
32. On what day did the Four Knights take ship for England?
33. What sort of meat do the Priests offer the Knights?
34. In which part of London was Thomas born?
35. Why does Thomas disclaim responsibility for "Suspending those who had crowned the young prince"?
36. Before leaving the Knights, after his first encounter with them, to which authority does Thomas submit his case?
37. What service do the Priests urge Thomas to attend?
38. What hymn is sung in Latin "by a choir in the distance" as the Chorus chants "Numb the hand and dry the eyelid"?
39. To what animals do the Priests liken the Four Knights?
40. What law, according to Thomas, is "above the Law of Man"?
41. To which part of the cathedral do the Priests urge Thomas to fly when the Knights come through the unbarred door?
42. Who, according to Thomas, is a "three times traitor"?
43. The name of which martyr is mentioned by Thomas as he is being butchered?
44. Who was the eldest of the Four Knights?
45. Who was the expert on "statecraft and constitutional law"?
46. Who were the rival rulers of England prior to the accession of Henry II?
47. What was the name of the Fourth Knight?

48. What, according to the Fourth Knight, "is the only charitable verdict" that can be given about Thomas's death?
49. Why do the Priests finally give thanks to God for Thomas's death?
50. What sort of hymn is sung in Latin "by a choir in the distance" during the chanting of the final chorus?

ANSWERS TO "TEST YOURSELF" QUESTIONS

(Page references are to the text published by Faber & Faber)
1. 2nd December, A.D. 1170 (9).
2. Seven years (12).
3. ". . . death from the sea" (12).
4. "A patched-up affair" (16).
5. "My Lord . . . I leave you as a man whom in this life I shall not see again" (16).
6. ". . . Frogs in the treetops" (21).
7. "Peace. And let them be, in their exaltation" (21).
8. "I will have fires laid in all your rooms" (12).
9. The Bishops of London and Salisbury (22).
10. Sandwich (22).
11. John, Dean of Salisbury (22).
12. "Friendship should be more than biting Time can sever" (24).
13. Twenty years (25).
14. Clarendon (26).
15. Northampton (26).
16. Montmirail, in Maine (26).
17. Second Tempter (27).
18. "A country-keeping lord who minds his own business" (31).
19. The Normans (32).
20. Angevins (32).
21. The barons (34).
22. Samson in Gaza (34).
23. His persecutors (39).
24. Death (42).
25. "To do the right deed for the wrong reason" (44)
26. Toulouse (44).
27. Saint Luke (47).
28. ". . . the blessed Stephen" (49).
29. Archbishop Elphege (50).
39. The owl (53).
31. The Second Priest (55).
32. 28th December (A.D. 1170) (57).

33. Roast pork (58).
34. Cheapside (59).
35. "It was (the Pope) who condemned them" (64).
36. "The judgement of Rome" (65).
37. Vespers (70).
38. A "Dies Irae" (70).
39. The lion, leopard, wolf and boar (73).
40. "The Law of God" (73).
41. The crypt (74).
42. Reginald FitzUrse (First Knight) (75).
43. St. Denys (76).
44. Baron William de Traci (Third Knight) (78)
45. Sir Hugh de Morville (Second Knight) (80).
46. Queen Matilda (Henry's mother) and Stephen (his uncle) (80).
47. Richard Brito (82).
48. That it was "Suicide while of unsound mind" (83).
49. Because God "has given us another saint in Canterbury" (85).
50. A "Te Deum" (85).

SOME GENERAL OBSERVATIONS

MARTYRDOM—THE CENTRAL THEME

ALTHOUGH the conflict between Church and State is a recurrent theme in the play, it never assumes major significance. Moreover, the clash of character and personal antagonisms is deliberately avoided: the king does not appear and the knights are at first not presented as individual characters but act as a gang; subsequently it is stressed that their actions have not been motivated by personal passions.

The central theme of the play is martyrdom, and Eliot's concept of martyrdom is the term as it was originally used. In its strict, ancient sense, the word martyr means witness, and the Church did not at first confine the term to those who had sealed their witnessing with their blood. So Becket as a martyr is not primarily one who suffers for a cause, or who gives up his life for some religious belief; instead, he is a witness to the reality of God's powers.

The actual deed by which Thomas is struck down is not important as a dramatic climax. The audience is warned again and again that it is not watching a sequence of events that contains the normal dramatic logic of motive, act, and result, but an action that depends on God's will and not on human behaviour.

Moreover, Thomas himself can hardly be said to be tempted, for the play opens so near its climax that the temptations are hardly more than recapitulations of things which have ceased to tempt him; and the last temptation (that he should *seek* martyrdom) is so subtle and subjective that no audience can really judge whether or not it is genuinely over-come. Although Thomas may say, "Now is my way clear, now is the meaning plain", a question has been raised that cannot be answered dramatically. We either have to accept Eliot's interpretation that Thomas dies with a pure will, or ignore the whole problem of motives as beyond our competence.

The martyr's sermon warns us that "a martyrdom is never the design of man", and that a Christian martyrdom is neither an accident nor "the effect of a man's will to become a saint". Becket has only to wait for his murderers to appear: "All my life they have been coming, these feet." When the knights rush the altar, the murder takes place as a kind of ritual slaughter of an unresisting victim, and this episode is not dramatically significant.

Accordingly, *Murder in the Cathedral* is not just a dramatization of the death of Becket; it is a deep-searching study of the significance of martyrdom. Historical detail is severely subordinated to this basic theme. Of the Archbishop's former career, Eliot incorporates only what is germane to his pattern of martyrdom, and that retrospectively through the first three temptations. What historical detail there is is skilfully used to point the main theme and relate it to the historical facts (e.g., the Second Tempter's speech on p. 26).

Throughout most of his career as a dramatist, Eliot has been preoccupied with the theme of spiritual election, though it is only in this play that sainthood is in the foreground. In his later plays, the theme has been pushed farther and farther into the background as he has sought to portray the contemporary world and show the relationship of sainthood and martyrdom to the lives of the ordinary men and women of today. But from the outset, to show this relationship was one of Eliot's chief aims as a dramatist.

DRAMATIC STRUCTURE

How, then, does martyrdom give *Murder in the Cathedral* its shape as well as its meaning?

Part I describes the temptations the martyr must undergo: first the temptations to compromise and avoid martyrdom; then the temptation to accept it in the wrong spirit, "to do the right deed for the wrong reason". The rest of Part I is constructed upon a strict, almost geometric, pattern, reaching its climax in a counterpointing of the temptations from within (the Tempters) and the claims of humanity from without (the Priests and the Chorus). The exchanges with the Tempters remain the focal point of the play. The first three recapitulate vices to which Thomas has been drawn earlier in his life, and are rejected with comparative ease. But the fourth is much more subtle, and ironically repeats Thomas's own words to the women of Canterbury, urging that affairs are out of his hands, and that he must merely adapt himself to fit the pattern imposed by God's will. The Chorus interrupts with a description of portents of disaster witnessed by them, demanding once more to be left to their spiritual apathy. So Thomas's answer to the Fourth Tempter, to spiritual pride and an aching desire for the glory of martyrdom, is delayed until the Chorus has spoken.

The sermon follows as an interlude between the two parts, giving expression to the self-knowledge that Becket has gained in Part I and showing him beginning to "make perfect (his) will" in readiness for the action of Part II. So, in the sermon, he analyses what exactly the wrong reason for martyrdom is, showing his insight into the ultimate betrayal suggested to him by defining the pattern of martyrdom, "the eternal design", in theological and emotional terms – in terms, that is, of the fulfilment of God's will and the testimony of mankind.

Part II begins with a device based on the liturgy as a means of rapidly and smoothly covering the passage of time from Christmas Day, on which the sermon is preached, to December 29th, the day of the martyrdom. The three Priests enter in procession, and, in turn, announce the passing of the days. The banners of the appropriate saints are carried in and the introits are heard. Through such devices much more than the mere passage of time is suggested: the idea of martyrdom and sainthood is kept before the audience.

Thereafter, the Knights, the "sordid" instruments of "the eternal design", burst into the scene, and the action from this point of the murder follows a comparatively realistic course. Then, the murder completed, the Knights step forward, drop into prose and complete informality of manner, and offer rationalizations for their action. Coming hard upon the agony of the martyr and the tremendous outburst of the Chorus in which tears "drown the wind", this abrupt transition is something midway between a political meeting and a music-hall act. Yet, the Knight's apologies remain an integral part of the play and are meant to shock the spectators out of sanctimonious complacency. Stepping out of their twelfth century setting, the Knights seek by every means from blandishment to exhortation, skilfully using the techniques of modern political oratory, to *tempt the audience* into admitting the reasonableness of their action and to acknowledge that they (the audience) are involved in it, since they have benefited from it.

Thereafter, for the Knights the play is over, and the First Knight suggests, in tones ironically echoing the words of policemen who have quelled a disturbance, "that you now disperse quietly to your homes" (p. 83). But the impact of Thomas's sacrifice remains: the Priests return and help to recover the mood of the martyrdom in a chastened form. From a threnody for the Archbishop in minor key, the recovered verse-form modulates to the major hymn of praise and thanksgiving for the new saint of Canterbury with which the play ends.

Hence, by cutting down the historical action to its bare essentials, Eliot has brought "the eternal design" into stark, dramatic relief.

CHARACTERIZATION OF ARCHBISHOP BECKET

Since *Murder in the Cathedral,* as shown above, is a study in the philosophical and religious aspects of martyrdom, there is very little room left for effective characterization. The Priests, Tempters, and Knights are symbols rather than flesh and blood creations and Eliot deliberately makes little effort to present them personally.

Even the character of Becket himself, around whom the whole action revolves, is a disappointment. His rôle is essentially a passive one: assailed by the Tempters, importuned by the Chorus, harassed by the Priests and murdered by the Knights, he has little to do but go forward to a predetermined fate. Nor is any of the best poetry in the play put into his mouth, while the long sermon in which he explains his slightly equivocal victory over spiritual pride is couched in such simple prose that it lacks dramatic impact.

Dramatic conciseness is achieved by confining the action of the play to the last days of Becket's life, the struggle within him being concentrated and given form in his talks with Tempters (a type of personification popular in the old mediaeval morality plays). From the words of the Tempters and of the Chorus we learn the bare facts of Thomas's early life, and of his former conflicts with the evils outside and within him. But all the time Eliot rejects many aspects of Becket's human qualities in order to select material for a portrait of a saint. (There is a tremendous contrast in the method used here with that employed, for example, by George Bernard Shaw in his portrayal of St. Joan.)

The dramatic problem, of course, is that the more perfect Eliot makes the saint's self-surrender the more difficult it becomes to keep him a real man, since it is in our weaknesses that our humanity is most apparent. Moreover, by confining the action of the play to the closing weeks of Becket's life and so forcing him to play a purely passive rôle, Eliot increases the difficulty of making Thomas entirely credible as a man (though he deepens the religious significance of the play).

There is more than a trace in the Archbishop of priggish behaviour which is somewhat disconcerting. There is a touch of professionalism about his sanctity; a note of complacency is always creeping into his self-conscious presentation of himself. He seems bent on showing everybody "how a Christian can die", and this attitude goes beyond the quality of insufferable pride — a quality which the audience is made aware of at an early stage by the words of the First Priest (pp. 16-17). There can be little doubt that Eliot conceived his hero as a superior person, but if there is no true action (if the centre of the play is a state of mind), this superiority can only be conveyed through self-conscious behaviour.

Some critics have gone so far as to compare Becket with Shakespeare's Macbeth, arguing that just as Macbeth is a noble character spoilt by ambition, so Becket is a noble character spoilt by pride. In fact, Eliot's approach reveals a contempt for personality and its expression in acts, and Thomas is less a man than an embodied attitude.

THE IMPACT OF THE CHORUS

While Eliot can be said to have failed to bring Becket to life (an inevitable failure in view of his emphasis on martyrdom as an aesthetic concept rather than as a manifestation of temperament), he scores a great success with the Chorus.

In a talk broadcast in the year after the production of *Murder in the Cathedral*, Eliot remarked that: "in making use of the Chorus we do not aim to copy Greek drama. There is a good deal about the Greek theatre that we do not know, and never shall know. But we know that some of its conventions cannot be ours . . . But the Chorus has always fundamentally the same uses. It mediates between the action and the audience; it intensifies the action by projecting its emotional consequences, so that we as the audience see it doubly, by seeing its effect on other people."

To this end, then, Eliot restored the full-throated chorus of ancient Greek tragedy after centuries of disuse. He has used the chorus to open out the action into its full significance, as nobody else has done since Aeschylus.

This Chorus provides one of the most challenging problems for a producer of the play. It speaks formal odes between scenes; it is deprived, as the Greek chorus was, of the right to participate in the action. Yet Eliot thinks of its members more as a group of individuals gripped by common emotions. To be successful, the Chorus of *Murder in the Cathedral* ought to be composed of women of widely differing ages, from one or two adolescents to women as old as can compass the extremely difficult task of learning lines in a chorus (far harder than when all your cues come from individuals and all your lines are yours alone). This means that to make the device work really well one must have a biggish group of women, each one of whom has some marked individual quality. It has also, technically, to be capable of a great variety of rhythm and of taking very long phrases in a single sweep. Emotionally, it has to be totally free from self-pity (the ultimate sin in acting) and free also from the *sound* of self-pity which is often due to lack of tonal control.

The women introduce themselves as "the poor, the poor women of

Canterbury" (p. 11), and later refer to themselves at their daily task as "the scrubbers and sweepers of Canterbury" (p. 86). They are "the small folk drawn into the pattern of fate, the small folk who live among small things" (p. 20). When we first see them, they have a premonition of what is to come and of their part in it, and they fear that they will not prove equal to the task (pp. 11-12). They fear even more the impending "disturbance of the quiet seasons", the irruption of the unknown, the uncontrollable, into the familiar round of their lives, which they have carefully ordered to create a feeling of security, conveniently forgetting what should make them question this false sense of safety and permanence. They would prefer "to pass unobserved". So, even though they recognize that what is about to happen is the design of God, they think of it as an illness, something they would rather do without.

To witness in the Christian sense means, however, not just to see but to be involved, to make a public avowal of faith in action as well as in words, and in their fear at the possible consequences of action they appeal rhetorically to Thomas and implore him to return to France (p. 20). As the Tempters gather their forces for a united attack on Thomas, the Chorus's fear mounts, through an oppressive sense of the evil at war with the good in him ("The earth is heaving to parturition of issue of hell", p. 41), to a sudden panic at the possibility that the "Lords of Hell" will triumph. They thus acknowledge that their spiritual welfare depends upon Thomas.

In the chorus which opens Part II, they admit the need for his sacrifice, but of their own part in the design (the consent implicit in standing by and doing nothing to prevent the murder) they are keenly ashamed ("Nothing is possible but the shamed swoon / Of those consenting to the last humiliation"). They have now consented to the "eternal patience" and acknowledged their responsibility for the imminent death of Thomas by recognizing that they will be involved in the sin of the murderers (p. 68). Even the evil of their timid inaction will be turned into a good for themselves and all men through the martyrdom which God has ordained.

As the moment of martyrdom approaches, however, the Chorus has a vision of horror of the Void as they picture the fate they can expect unless atonement is made. From it the women turn to the comfort of Christ's sacrifice about to be renewed in the martyrdom of Thomas. By the end of the play they have arrived at a full understanding of the significance of Thomas's death. They experience the moment of "painful joy" prophesied by Thomas (pp. 68-9) and acknowledge that his sacrifice was made on their behalf (p. 88). Thus, under the impact of the martyrdom, they have moved from apathy and evasion to a lively faith and humble acceptance.

The Chorus, then, provides both background and counterpoint to the action, and it is through its reaction to the events of the martyrdom of Thomas, through its opposition and final reconciliation, that the tension and very powerful atmosphere are built up and maintained.

VERSE AND LANGUAGE

It is the power of the dramatic verse that gives the play its unique quality of unity and intensity. "The language is the verse, which is the action, which is the theme, which is the atmosphere, which is the meaning" (Séan Lucy, *T. S. Eliot and the Idea of Tradition,* p. 187). In other words, the play is an impressive realization of the dramatic potentials which Eliot himself, in his critical works, has claimed for verse.

Being at no pains to hide the fact that he was writing in verse – indeed, being inclined to obtrude the verse-form upon the audience – Eliot employs a variety of metres as well as two stretches of prose. He develops a style suitable to each kind of scene. The most superficial level, that of the quarrels between Becket and the Knights, is no more than rhymed doggerel. More subtle, and sometimes rather crabbed, is a four-stress rhyming verse for the Tempters who dramatize the tortuous progress of Becket's inner struggle. There is free verse for dialogue with the Priests and Chorus, and for the Chorus itself, a very varied series of forms, from the three-stress lines of the women's domestic talk to the long complexes of pleading or of praise. In addition, Eliot uses the rhythms of two mediaeval hymns as ground-bass of choral odes.

Again, it is with the Chorus that Eliot is poetically most successful. The choruses owe much to the rhythms of Biblical verse (especially the psalter) with its simplicity of syntax, emphatic repetitions, and rhythmical variety. It is important to observe in this connection the difference between the metres of dialogue and choral metres. Choric speaking must be emphatic or the sense is lost: it must keep time, and cannot indulge in too much variation of speed and tone. Many voices speaking together are incapable of the subtle modulations of a single voice, and of the innumerable variations from a regular metrical base that make up the music of poetry. On the other hand, if the metre is too regular, choral speaking will soon reduce it to the monotony of sing-song. Choric verse must therefore itself be written in free metres; the necessary variety must be inherent in the metrical structure, in variation in the length of line, and the length of the breath units. In short, where verse-dialogue approximates to speech, choric verse must approximate to chant.

35

TYPICAL EXAMINATION QUESTIONS

NOTE: The following are some revision exercises and typical questions which might be asked on *Murder in the Cathedral* in an examination. It must be stressed, however, that a thorough familiarity with the text itself is essential to achieve good marks in such an examination, and that these questions are *not* to be considered as likely "spots".

CONTENT QUESTIONS

1. Give an account of the exchanges between Chorus, Priests, and Messenger before Becket's arrival in Canterbury.

2. Describe the conversations between Thomas and the first three Tempters.

3. Recount the visit of the Fourth Tempter and show why he is more significant to the unfolding of the drama than his three predecessors.

4. What part is played by the Priests in *Murder in the Cathedral*? Is any effort made to give them individual personalities?

5. With the aid of brief, appropriate quotations, give an outline of Thomas's sermon in Canterbury Cathedral on Christmas Day.

6. Although King Henry II never appears in the play in person, what does the audience learn of the course of the quarrel between the King and Archbishop?

7. Give an account of the arguments between the Knights and Thomas from the time of their first encounter with him until their murder of the Archbishop.

8. Summarize the main points made by the Knights in their speeches after Thomas's murder.

9. What are the principal emotions expressed by the Chorus in the two chants beginning (a) "I have smelt them, the death-bringers . . .", and (b) "Clear the air! clean the sky! wash the wind! . . ."?

10. What information is given in the course of the play about:
    (a) Becket's former career;
    (b) the condition of the common people?

11. "If in the first act the strife is with shadows, in the second there is no strife at all."
Do you agree with this assessment of the degree of dramatic conflict to be found in *Murder in the Cathedral*? State your reasons fully.

12. "To put expressions of humility into a man's mouth is to risk making him appear the opposite of humble."
"A note of complacency is always creeping into Thomas's self-conscious presentation of himself."
To what extent do you agree with the implications of these two criticisms of Eliot's character-portrayal of Becket?

13. Write explanatory notes on *each* of the following:
    (a) the use of Biblical imagery;
    (b) the verse-forms employed in the play;
    (c) the introduction of church ritual.

14. "There are in fact three motifs in *Murder in the Cathedral,* not intertwined but competing for prominence: the change in the orientation of Becket's will; the strike between secularism and the will of God; and the death of a valiant man."
Discuss the implications of this assertion.

15. "*Murder in the Cathedral* is not just a dramatization of the death of Thomas Becket; it is a deep-searching study of the significance of martyrdom."
To what extent does the concept of martyrdom dominate the whole atmosphere and action of the play?

16. With the aid of brief, appropriate quotations, trace the extent to which the views and emotions of the Chorus undergo transformation during the course of the play.

17. "The Wheel of Life and the Will of God both bear Becket toward the same violent death; they determine, however, whether that death will belong to the world's categories, murder or even suicide, or whether it will constitute a martyrdom enjoyed by God's love."
To what extent does Eliot successfully resolve the main moral implication of the play, the purification of Becket's will?

18. "The figure of Becket, as it emerges in *Murder in the Cathedral,* is passive, negative, and completely lacking in emotional intensity."
Do you agree with this assessment? State your reasons fully.

37

19. Read the following passage carefully and then answer the questions below:

"Your Lordship has forgotten me, perhaps. I will remind you.
We met at Clarendon, at Northampton,
And last at Montmirail, in Maine. Now that I have recalled them,
Let us but set these not too pleasant memories
In balance against other, earlier
And weightier ones: those of the Chancellorship.
See how the late ones rise! You, master of policy
Whom all acknowledged, should guide the state again."

(a) Who speaks these words and what does the speaker symbolize or represent?
(b) What had happened at (i) Clarendon, (ii) Northampton, and (iii) Montmirail?
(c) Why should mention of the Chancellorship recall pleasant memories?
(d) What will Thomas have to do in order to "guide the state again"?
(e) How does Becket react to this offer of the Chancellorship?
(f) Comment on the verse-form in this passage.

20. For *each* of the following quotations, (i) identify the speaker or speakers, (ii) describe the specific circumstances in which the words are spoken, and (iii) comment briefly on the significance of the words to the play in general.

(a) "You are hard-headed sensible people as I can see, and not to be taken in by emotional clap-trap. I therefore ask you to consider soberly: what were the Archbishop's aims? and what are King Henry's aims? In the answer to these questions lies the key to the problem."

(b) "You are right to express a certain incredulity.
He comes in pride and sorrow, affirming all his claims,
Assured, beyond doubt, of the devotion of the people,
Who receive him with scenes of frenzied enthusiasm,
Lining the road and throwing down their capes,
Strewing the way with leaves and late flowers of the season."

(c) "I offer what you desire. I ask
What you have to give. Is it too much
For such a vision of eternal grandeur?"

(d) "Now is my way clear, now is the meaning plain:
Temptation shall not come in this kind again.
The last temptation is the greatest treason:

38

To do the right deed for the wrong reason."

(e) "My Lord, they are coming. They will break through presently.
You will be killed. Come to the altar.
Make haste, my Lord. Don't stop here talking. It is not right.
What shall become of us, my Lord, if you are killed; what shall
    become of us?"

The above quotations will be found on the following pages of the
fourth edition of *Murder in the Cathedral* published by Faber & Faber:
19, p. 26; 20, (a) p. 80; (b) p. 15; (c) p. 39; (d) p. 44; (e) p. 69.

Section IX

BIBLIOGRAPHICAL NOTES

FOR a brief introduction to the literary career of T. S. Eliot the student should consult the short monograph on the author by M. C. Bradbrook (published by Longmans, Green & Co. for the British Council); all of Eliot's own poetry and prose work is published by Messrs. Faber & Faber, though there is a paperback selection of the poems in the Penguin series.

A good deal of critical commentary has been written about Eliot as poet and dramatist, of which the following recent works are particularly useful: Hugh Kenner, *The Invisible Poet* (W. H. Allen, 1960), Séan Lucy, *T. S. Eliot and the Idea of Tradition* (Cohen & West, 1960), and D. E. Jones, *The Plays of T. S. Eliot* (Routledge & Kegan Paul, 1960).

In addition, on *Murder in the Cathedral* itself, the following learned journals contain interesting material (though some of it is at the university rather than the school level of discussion): Patricia Adair, *Mr. Eliot's "Murder in the Cathedral"*, The Cambridge Journal, Vol. IV, No. 2 (November, 1950), pp. 83-95; Louis L. Martz, *The Wheel and the Point: Aspects of Imagery and Theme in Eliot's later Poetry*, The Sewanee Review, LV (1947), pp. 126-147; Leo Shapiro, *The Medievalism of T. S. Eliot*, Poetry, Vol. LVI, No. 4 (July 1940).

For the historical setting of the play and the clash between Becket and Henry II, a useful summary will be found in Christopher Brooke, *From Alfred to Henry III* (Nelson's History of England, Vol. II, 1961); see also the various chapters on clerical, social, and economic life in *Medieval England*, 2 vols. (A. L. Poole, ed., Oxford University Press, 1958).

D1634837